Take and

A GUIDE TO THE BIBLE
FOR LAY READERS

Billy FitzGerald

Take and Read

A GUIDE TO THE BIBLE
FOR LAY READERS

DOMINICAN PUBLICATIONS

First published (1993) by
Dominican Publications
42 Parnell Sqaure
Dublin 1

ISBN 1-871552-40-0

Cover design by
David Cooke

Printed in Ireland by
Colour Books Ltd, Baldoyle, Dublin 13

Contents

	Introduction	1
1	Understanding the Origins	5
2	A Whole Library	9
3	Search for Salvation	13
4	The Books of Moses	19
5	The Prophets	22
6	The Psalms	26
7	Between the Testaments	32
8	Paul	36
9	Three Gospels	41
10	The Fourth Gospel	46
11	The Sources	50
12	Biblical Truth	57
13	Getting It Right	61
14	Reading the Prayer of the Faithful	67
15	Pronounciation Guide	70

The ministry of reader

Reading in church is not a task; it is a ministry. And, like all ministries, it needs to be worked at. This work cannot just begin when a frantic curate or sacristan collars someone just before Mass begins and thrusts a missalette into their hands. That is not fair to anybody – the reader, the congregation or even God himself! So, where must we begin? Why not at the beginning: 'In the beginning was the Word, and the Word was with God, and the Word was God'.

Like it or not, that is where we are – caught up in the business of bringing the living Word of God to his people. This really is an awesome thing to be asked to do. But that is how God has chosen to work. His Word is to be proclaimed to people, by people, until the end of time. And it is up to us to carry out that task in this place and at this time.

So, it seems that we have no choice but to do it well; as well as possible, for we have a responsibility both to God and to his people.

This means, first of all, that there must be a proper preparation. Preparation is perhaps the most important notion for all readers. But what kind of preparation? Preparation of *ourselves*. The prayer of the centurion would not be a bad start; 'Lord, I am not worthy ... ' and, after that, constantly, a prayer for help and guidance. At least, if we are prepared to pray about our ministry as readers, it is unlikely that we will forget that we are not in this alone. We are part of a team which includes the Lord himself.

After prayer, the next most important kind of preparation is study. We have got to know our Bible and we have got to know *about* our Bible. Only out of this comes understanding. And understanding is what it is all about. God's message has a meaning, and that meaning must be understood by the reader and then passed on to those who are listening. Without understanding on the part of the reader, the meaning will be lost and the church will be filled with nothing but the sound of words.

Therefore, every reader needs two tools of the trade, so to speak. The first is, of course, their own copy of the Bible. This should be carefully chosen. It should, ideally, be the same translation or version as is used in church on Sunday. It should have print that is big enough to read comfortably. Small print is tiring and tiresome. It is important that the Bible be your own so that, if need be, you are free to pencil the occasional note in the margin, or underline a key phrase. The second tool of the trade is what is commonly called a commentary. This is simply a book which takes each chapter and verse of the Scriptures and explains its background and meaning. Choice of a suitable commentary is probably best done in consultation with your parish clergy or study group leader.

Armed with Bible and commentary, we are now in business! We can, with a modicum of care, establish the meaning of any passage of Scripture that we may be asked to read.

At the lectern itself, how are we to read? The simple answer is, clearly. Clarity is the key. The hurried word and the mumbled word have no meaning. And one of the greatest enemies of clarity is speed. Most newcomers to reading in church read too quickly. This is understandable if we are nervous. But nervousness soon disappears, especially if we have prepared well, because preparation gives confidence. Remember, we are not up there at the lectern for our own sake. The important thing is not so much ourselves but the message from God that has been entrusted to us for handing on to his people today.

Hustle and bustle do nothing for his message either. There is a world of difference between the reader who scurries to the lectern, unfolding a crumpled missalette on the way there, and the reader who takes his or her place calmly and reads distinctly and with dignity from the lectionary.

The Second Vatican Council, in its Constitution on the Liturgy, urged that the sacred Scriptures should be made more available to the faithful. The Bible is special, but not so special that it should be locked away in libraries, for the eyes of scholars only!

As a result, the lectionary was drawn up. The lectionary itself takes a little understanding: it is not the whole Bible. The word 'lectionary' simply means a list or collection of those extracts from the Bible for use during worship.

The choice of which passages to use has been made with a view to the general mood and atmosphere of the various seasons of the Church year. Thus, for example, the readings for Advent will feature the prophecies of the coming Messiah. Similarly, Christmas, Easter and Pentecost will have their own particular slant or orientation.

Because there are only fifty two Sundays in the year, a limiting factor, the Sunday lectionary is divided into three 'cycles' or sets of readings. This means that we get a much wider selection of biblical extracts than would be possible with a one-year cycle. Now we come back to the beginning only once in every three years.

On a normal Sunday there are three selections made: one reading from the Old Testament, one from the Epistles of the New Testament, and one from the Gospels. The choice of extracts from the Gospels is determined by the year; for example in 1994 the Gospels are mainly from Saint Mark; from Luke in 1995 and Matthew in 1996, coming back to Mark in 1997, and so on. Selections from Saint John's Gospel are used on certain Sundays of each year.

The reading of God's word at Mass is far too important to be left to anything like chance. Many bishops insist that before anyone is called to be a Special Minister of the Eucharist they must receive some basic training both in eucharistic theology and in the practical skills necessary. Ideally, Ministers of the Word would best be prepared by a similar arrangement.

Some of the material in this book appeared originally in more expanded form in an earlier work, *Bestseller*, published by RTÉ. I am grateful for permission to use it.

References
The Constitution on the Liturgy is available in Austin Flannery OP (editor) *Vatican Council II: Conciliar and Post-Conciliar Documents*, Dublin. Dominican Publications, 1992 edition.

ONE

Understanding the origins

The Bible is probably the most widely read book in the world. There are about two thousand million copies of it in circulation, and a further two million join them every year. It has been published in as many as twelve hundred different languages, and is available today in anything from the original Hebrew and Greek to Irish, English, or the language of the Kadazans of North Borneo. Wherever missionaries have gone, one of their first tasks has been to translate the Scriptures into the local language.

It is clear that this book has, for centuries, held a fascination for millions of people. Why is this? It certainly is not because it makes for easy reading. In fact, some parts of it are so difficult and obscure that they can only be understood after considerable study. Yet the Bible also contains some of the most beautiful and sublime literature ever written.

The next question, then, must be whether it has anything to offer an enlightened twentieth century. Certainly, we hear sections of it read in our churches Sunday after Sunday. But, if some of the things we hear read out are to make sense, we need to know more about the Bible and where it came from in the first place.

If we treat the Bible like any other book, picking it up, starting at page one and going straight on from there, we are bound to flounder or get lost. It is not meant to the read that way.

Where do we start, then? How will it make the best sense? The best way, probably is to start not with the story of creation (as found in Genesis, chapter one), but with the story of one man, Abram. Abram lived about as far distant in time from

Christ as we do: about two thousand years. Tradition tells us that he was a tribesman, a member of the clan of Terah, living in a place called Ur in Mesopotamia. The clan left Ur and led a nomadic life on the fringes of what has come to be called the Fertile Crescent.

This was a sweep of fertile land curving from the Persian Gulf in the East, up the course of the Tigris and Euphrates rivers, through what today are Syria and Jordan, and eventually ending up on the Mediterranean coast of Egypt. Abram's people lived on the edge of this sweep of land where they could graze their flocks on the scutch-grass that grows at the edge of the desert.

Not everybody in those days was a wanderer. Most of the inhabitants of the Fertile Crescent lived in the cities that made up the Babylonian Empire. These people were highly civilized and sophisticated. Their cities really were great; their ruins are to be seen to this day. They had their streets and their markets; their municipal buildings; their court-houses and temples, for they were a religious people; and they had their libraries.

What was in these libraries? Books? Yes, but not books that we would immediately recognize as such. The invention of paper had not yet reached Babylonia. Instead, their writing was done in tablets of dried clay. And some of their most important documents were religious: accounts of creation, of great gods and goddesses, of the struggle between good and evil, and even accounts of a great flood.

The gods of the Fertile Crescent were worshipped in shrines which were built on top of huge artificial mountains. These massive constructions were called *ziggurats*, and were comparable as engineering feats to the pyramids of Egypt. Their origins are lost in the mists of pre-history.

This was the world of Abram. But, as we can read in the Book of Genesis, chapter twelve, Abram was to make the break from the worship of these gods. In a passage that is extraordinary because it seems so casual, we are told how a new God suddenly revealed himself to Abram. In a series of revelations, this new God tells Abram how he wants to be worshipped. There are to be no more human sacrifices. In a dramatic test of faith that is at the same time an object-lesson, God stays Abram's hand as he is about to offer the life of his own son. And this new God speaks to Abram as a friend and not as a tyrant to be appeased like the other tribal gods.

In another dramatic move, God tells Abram that he is about to change his name from Abram (which means Great Father) to Abraham (which means Father of a Multitude). Abraham was to become the leader of a whole nation! This must have been a traumatic experience for someone who had been no more than a fairly simple man: local chieftain of a comparatively small tribe. But it is the beginning of our story.

The whole history of Abraham and his family; their journeys, their battles, their celebrations and their worship; the history of their descendants, Isaac, Jacob, and Joseph; their eventual reduction to slavery in Egypt; their escape under the leadership of a man called Moses – all this originally was not in written form at all. It was simply an unwritten tradition, handed down by word of mouth in story and song from generation to generation around desert camp-fires for literally hundreds of years.

Eventually, however, all these stories were gathered together, put in order and written down. But this happened very slowly. More than a thousand years were to pass after the time of Abraham and the other Patriarchs before the stories about them reached anything like the form we now recognize in the Book of Genesis.

In a sense, then, it is something of a wonder that the story of those people has reached us at all. But it has come down to us, although not originally in one book between one set of covers, but as a collection of widely different documents.

TWO

A whole library

The Bible began as little more than a few inscribed clay or 'stone' tablets and a great body of folklore, camp-fire tales, and indeed *Credos* – acts of faith in a God who was seen as revealing himself in the course of human history. This body of folk culture was preserved and recalled for generations by the Semitic nomads wandering in the desert fringes of the area we have called the Fertile Crescent, lying between the Persian Gulf and the Mediterranean Sea.

How long could such fragmentary folklore have survived in this way? How long was it, in fact, until it got written down? Before we can even begin to answer those questions there is one idea that we must get rid of completely: the idea that the Bible is a single book. It is not. We, at our stage of history, are spoiled. The Bible usually comes to us neatly packaged between one set of covers, and printed in one language, all neat and compact. So, we have got used to thinking of the Bible as *a* book. But it is not just one book. It is really a collection of books, articles, letters and poems, composed, written down, and collected over the course of thousands of years, by many different people who lived in what we now call Egypt, Israel, Jordan, Syria, Lebanon, Iran, Iraq, and Saudi Arabia. So, if we ask, 'What *is* the Bible?', we are asking the wrong question. More correctly, if ungrammatically, the question is, 'What *are* the Bible?' Thus we can go on to find out more about these writings, and see how it is that many different books can form a unity, and what it is that justifies us putting them between the same set of covers and giving them one blanket title.

For Christians, the books that make up the Bible are divided into two separate collections: the ones that were written before the time of Christ, and those that were written after him. The parts are not equal. There is about four times as much material from the time before Christ as there is from the time after him. So, this is our first division of material. The writings that existed before Christ Christians call the Old Testament. The later ones, which are largely written about Christ, we call the New Testament. One meaning of the word 'testament' itself is a bearing of witness' to something. To what? Both testaments bear witness to the history of God's contact with humankind and humankind's contact with God: God revealing himself to our race, and our response to that revelation.

In the Bible, the word 'testament' has many shades of meaning: it refers not just to bearing witness but to the special Covenant between God and his people. In the books of the Old Testament, the Covenant is, again and again, expressed in the terms, 'I will be your God and you shall be my people'. Recognition of this special relationship between God and his people was often celebrated by the offering of a sacrifice. In the New Testament, we see Jesus taking up the Old Testament terminology, and showing himself to his disciples as the mediator of the new Covenant between God and his people. 'I am your God and your are my people' is the awesome truth recalled every time we celebrate the Eucharist.

But let us get back to an earlier question: When did it all get written down? It probably happened shortly after the death of King David. He reigned from about the year 1050 B.C. until 975 B.C. When he died, an unknown scribe wrote down his story, probably on a vellum or parchment scroll. Such scrolls were reserved for very special documents. Today similar scrolls are written out by hand for use in Jewish synagogue worship. The text is written on separate sheets, two columns at a time, and then the sheets are stitched together. A scroll containing the

Pentateuch, that is the first five books of the Bible, can measure up to sixteen feet when fully rolled out. It takes scribes many weeks, working with pen and ink, to complete such a scroll.

It was probably on such a scroll that the history of the reign of King David was written. That would have been done about nine hundred years before the birth of Christ, and a good thousand years after the time of Abraham. Even then writing was only for special things. Apart from a few bits and scraps of writing, the religious traditions of the people had been kept in their heads for well on a thousand years, and indeed for many years afterwards. It was only the extremely important people and events that would have been written about. What does survive is only in the form of bits and scraps. Out of this kind of bitty jig-saw puzzle, how on earth can we realistically hope to reconstruct a whole Bible, the youngest piece of which must be at least seventeen hundred years old? We can start by reminding ourselves that the Bible is not so much a single book as a whole collection of books. And these are not even all the same kind of book.

Go into any library. If you do not know the basic distinction between fact and fiction, or between history and drama, between poetry and prose, then you will not be able to make much sense of the library. Still less could you make sense of a collection as old and as strange as the Bible. In the Bible, as in a library, we find many kinds of writing: poetry and prose, prayers and psalms, a romantic novel, and a particularly difficult kind of writing called Apocalypse which is very florid and visionary in style and which needs particularly careful attention.

The Book of Psalms is made up of poems and songs about God and the world he created. Traditionally, these were regarded as the work of the great King David, who was both a poet and a musician, although some of the psalms were in fact written long after his time. Psalm 77 is a good example of how the psalmist meditated on the wonderful things God has done for his people.

The books of the Bible are the work of many different authors writing in the course of centuries. And yet, different as they are, there is one thing that knits them together: whenever we read from any of them in our liturgies we say, 'This is the word of the Lord'. God, the same God who revealed himself to Abraham, is seen to be in some way responsible for them all. We believe that God not only spoke in some way to our ancestors in the faith, but actually speaks to us too in our day, through this very unusual collection of literary bits and pieces. As a result, almost all Jewish and Christian acts of worship are built up from texts of the Scriptures.

There are two very important and distinct things involved here: the notion of *revelation* (God speaking his truth to us), and the idea of *inspiration* (God somehow causing human writers to express what he wants said). We cannot really understand the Scriptures unless we have some understanding of these two key notions. How God can operate through human agents in this way, without doing violence to the writers, will always remain something of a mystery.

The ultimate act of God's self-revelation, however, was not a *written* word at all, but rather a person: the man, Jesus Christ, whom, with the help of the gift of faith, Christians recognize to be the focus not only of the New Testament, but also of the things that were said and done among the Hebrews during the two thousand years before his birth and which are chronicled in the pages of the Old Testament.

THREE

Search for salvation

Running through the books of the Bible is the belief that in a special way they are the 'Word of the Lord'. They proclaim the belief that there is a God and that he speaks to his people. This God, by intervening in human history, promises something called 'salvation' or, in other words, rescue. But rescue from what? That often depends on who is writing and under what circumstances. Sometimes it is rescue from the threat of surrounding tribes. Sometimes it is rescue from captivity when these tribes have been successful and taken their victims off into exile and, often, slavery. Sometimes it is rescue from evil in general: suffering disease or even sin. This rescue, or salvation, is seen, first of all, in human terms: a great leader will come, a politician, a general, or a king. Or maybe it will not be an individual, but rather a whole series, a succession, of leaders.

For the four hundred years between 1600 B.C. and 1200 B.C., the descendants of Abraham, Isaac and Jacob lived in Egypt where they had originally been driven by famine. Under the rule of the Pharaohs they were eventually reduced to the status of second class citizens, until ultimately they were no more than slaves. The massive rock-temples of Abu Simbel, recently rescued (by a massive international effort) from the risk of inundation, were built by the Pharaoh Rameses II, who came to the Egyptian throne in the year 1301 B.C. Rameses were obsessed by the notion of leaving behind a worthy monument to himself after his death. The facade of one of the Abu Simbel temples is decorated with four sixty-foot statues of himself. For an absolute ruler who is intent on this sort of self-glorification there is only one way to get the work done – by slaves. The Hebrews in Egypt in the twelfth century B.C. did not just know the temples of Abu Simbel to see. The likelihood is that they reluctantly helped to build them, and under conditions of extreme harassment, as when they were forced to manufacture their daily quota of dried-clay bricks without the normal binding agent of straw. Such a frustrating experience was naturally explosive and could not last. The Israelites needed a leader who would organise and co-ordinate an escape. As it turned out, that leader was a man called Moses.

Like so many great people of history, Moses' origins are mysterious. He was born some three hundred years before any of the great stories about him was written down. Even his name, Moses, is interesting. He was born in Egypt, and his name was a common Egyptian one, not a Hebrew name. Nevertheless he was to become the representative of God before the Chosen People. It is ironic, then, that this great hero and leader may not have been a Hebrew at all, but an Egyptian, possibly born of an Egyptian father and a Jewish mother.

However, whatever his origins, Moses was just the man to stand up to Pharaoh. Through a whole series of threats and negotiations, he eventually led his people out of Egypt and out of slavery, across the Nile and the Red Sea into the Negev desert, where they wandered for forty years. At the end of that time, when they eventually entered the Promised Land, they were a sorry, scattered bunch. Moses himself died before that day dawned. As he was dying, they brought him to the top of Mount Nebo from where he could see the Promised Land in the distance. There he died and was buried.

So, eventually, the Hebrews crossed the Jordan, in their twelve tribes, and settled in the land of Canaan. Not that the local inhabitants made them particularly welcome. There was still a fairly rough time ahead. There were to be constant skirmishes with the surrounding tribesmen. And now there was no longer a Moses to bind them together and to lead them. But the Lord raised up for them new local tribal leaders, whom they called the Judges. For a blow-by-blow account of their adventures you should read that part of the Bible called the Book of Judges.

By the year 1035 B.C. the Israelites had settled down in their own land. The age of the Judges was over, and we find them being ruled by kings of their own, such as Saul, David and Solomon who built the temple at Jerusalem. And it is during this time, especially in the reign of King David, that we get the development of a new idea: that God chooses special people to be the guides, protectors and rulers of his people. These were to be called the 'Anointed Ones', a very important title, as we shall see.

At that time, the land of Canaan was clothed with olive groves. Olive oil was used both for cooking and for lighting, Oil was, therefore, one of the Israelites' main exports. Priests and prophets used this oil to anoint the heads of kings as a sign of their divine mission to guide the people. The Hebrew word, *mashia*, means 'anointed one'. And so we get our word, *Messiah*. The word grew to mean someone who was appointed to set up God's rule, his kingdom, among men and women. This started off, understandably, very much as a political notion. If we want to understand what it meant for the Israelites, we have to be careful not to read into it the later Christian meaning of the word, Messiah, which is much more a spiritual one.

In the year 581 B.C. came a great disaster. King Nebuchadnezzar of Babylon invaded, took and destroyed Jerusalem. To the Hebrews this was like the end of the world. From then until the year 538 B.C. – approximately fifty years – they were exiles in Babylon. By the year 538 B.C., Babylon itself had been taken over by the Persians, and the new king, Cyrus, made an edict allowing the Jews to return to their own land. The following twenty-five years they spent re-building their nation, their city, and especially their temple.

In this, once again, they had the help of a stranger, a Persian called Nehemiah. Not only did he get the walls of the city re-built in record time, fifty-seven days, but he also re-established worship in the temple. He closed the shops that were in business on the Sabbath, and made a public exhibition of some VIPs who had broken the law and married wives from surrounding tribes. He was a tough man, especially on matters of mixed marriages. But the people listened to him and got things done. He was just what they needed, a good, strong leader. But Nehemiah was only on loan. Eventually he had to go back to the court of King Cyrus. The Jews still lacked the one thing they needed: a leader of their own, an anointed one, a Messiah.

In this way, the idea of a search for a leader of their own, divinely appointed, who would deliver them from whatever the current crisis was, became one of the key ideas running through the whole of Jewish history.

Meantime, Rome was on the move. The great Roman general, Pompey, extending the Roman Empire with its trade all around the Mediterranean, arrived at Jerusalem in the year 63 B.C. He took the Holy Land, and Judea became part of the Roman Empire. A puppet-king was appointed, but the territory was really ruled from Rome, through a governor. Herod was such a puppet-king, Pilate such a governor. The Jewish people needed, once again, a liberator, a Messiah.

Just at this time, a generation after the arrival of Roman rule, at a place called Bethlehem, which had once been King David's city, a child was born to the wife of a man called Joseph who, tradition says, was a carpenter. The child's name was Joshua, or Jesus. When he grew up he went north to live near the Sea of Galilee. There he started to preach and proclaim the setting up of a New Kingdom. His preaching was done in both the 'official' setting of the local synagogues and in the open air, on the hillsides and the beaches, where he would, at times, attract an audience as large as five thousand. Among his followers he picked out twelve whom he called apostles, a word which actually means ambassadors. These he schooled in a special way for a task which, at the time, they hardly understood at all.

It was not just a matter of preaching. Wonderful signs accompanied the words of Jesus and of the apostles. The blind came to see, the lame walked, the deaf heard, and even the dead were brought back to life. This went on for three years at least. During this time, Jesus built up quite a following in Galilee. But when he ventured south to the centre of power, Jerusalem, the authorities had little trouble in putting him down. He was written off as an upstart, a would-be messiah, and executed.

Then strange things started to happen. His followers began to claim that he had been raised from the dead. He who had brought others back to life had been killed, and was now alive himself. His followers spoke and preached with enormous enthusiasm. He became for them the fulfilment of the messianic hopes. Perhaps, after all, the Messiah had come. Peter (in St Luke's Gospel) had proclaimed Jesus as 'the Christ of God'. For Christians this is a very important title. The Gospels, as they have come down to us, were written in Greek. And the Greek word, *Christos*, or Christ, is the equivalent of the Hebrew, *Meshia*, the Messiah, or the Anointed One. So, in this incident, Peter is giving Jesus the title of Messiah.

And what does Jesus do? He commanded them to tell this to no one, saying that he must suffer many things, be rejected by the elders and chief priests, suffer death, and on the third day be raised from the dead. Why did he forbid them to proclaim him as Messiah? Perhaps it was because the word 'messiah' by that time had become too political in meaning. If he was their

Messiah, he was a strange one. Although he had been born in Royal David's city, nevertheless he was not royal or noble in the accepted sense. He did not set up a political kingdom. He had not been visibly victorious over his enemies. Quite the opposite was the case. They had been victorious over him. He had not delivered Jerusalem from Roman occupation, which was the least any self-respecting Messiah could have been expected to do. And he certainly had not subjected the world of the Gentiles to the rule of God. In no way could he be the Messiah they had been expecting.

Yet, for Christians, Jesus is the Messiah. Just how he came to be recognized as such we shall see in a later chapter. But if he can be recognized as the Messiah, then the constant hope of a redeemer, which runs right through the Old Testament, can be seen to point to him. He is the focus of both the Old Testament and the New. This small-time carpenter, friend of down-and-outs, and failed politician, who was executed for his teaching, is the focal point and key of our whole Bible.

FOUR

The Books of Moses

The Bible, then, is not a single book, but rather a collection of about seventy different writings from many different ages and origins. Christians divide these writings into two collections, the Old Testament and the New. Among the books that make up the Old Testament there are five that deserve special mention. They are often given the Greek collective title of 'The *Pentateuch*'. These are the first five books we find when we open our Bibles.

It does not follow, of course, that they were the first five to be written. But they are special, and they belong together. Among the Jews they were called the five books of the Law or the *Torah*, or, again, the Five Fifths, meaning that they were understood to contain the whole of God's Law as revealed to Moses: the whole law of life. In fact, so special were these books to the people of Samaria that for them these five books alone *are* the Bible. They do not recognise any of the other books. Visitors to their synagogue in Samaria even today see an ancient and highly venerated scroll which contains just these five books.

Between them these five books contain many of the traditional Bible stories. The first of these books is the Book of Genesis. It tells the stories of Creation, the Fall, Cain and Abel, the Flood, the Tower of Babel, and Abraham. This book, in the main, is made up of two distinct traditions, one much older than the other, both telling the same truths but in different ways. That is why it contains, for instance, two distinct accounts of creation. Genesis alone raises a whole host of questions about the created world and modern science, which we will deal with in Chapter Thirteen.

The second book of the Pentateuch is the Book of Exodus. The word, 'exodus', itself simply means a 'going out'. You could call this book *The Great Escape*, telling, as it does, how Moses led the Hebrews out of their slavery in Egypt and about their forty years of wandering in the Sinai desert. Exodus has provided the material for many a massive motion picture: The Bible according to Cecil B. de Mille and many of his disciples who, between them, surely made the Red Sea do things that Moses and his followers never saw it do.

After Exodus come the two books of Leviticus and Numbers. These also deal with the life of Moses, and particularly with the details of how the God who revealed himself on Mount Sinai wanted to be worshipped.

The last book of these five is called Deuteronomy. The word means a 'second telling' of the Law of God. In it we find one important element that was not in the previous books. It shows God not as tyrant, as many of the non-Jewish tribes of those times saw their gods, but as a loving God who gives his laws and his promise as a protection and a blessing. The God of the Book of Deuteronomy is a loving and caring God.

The books of the Pentateuch were given their final shape between the years 900 and 400 B.C. The truths which they contain, however, are much older, and reading them we find that what they say is as relevant today as ever it was.

An ancient tradition says that Moses was the author of these five books. And even though we know that he could not have written them all with his own hand, it is true that they are his books in the sense that he is by far the most significant figure featured in them. He was the great liberator of his people. He led them out, not just across the Sinai desert, but into a new and more intimate knowledge of God, *their* God. Through him humankind reached a new and spectacular intimacy with God.

This friendship between God and the human race was symbolised and summed up in the setting up of the Covenant. This was a solemn agreement in which God said. 'I will be your God and you will be my people'. Nowhere else in the history of primitive religions will you find a god who speaks to men and women in the language of love as our God speaks to Moses, his people, and eventually to us in the pages of the Scriptures. The great Covenant was ritually celebrated, year after year, both during the wanderings in the desert and later, in the elaborate ceremonies of the temple when at last the wanderings ended and the Israelites had reached Jerusalem.

FIVE

The prophets

'Charismatic' is a word which is often seriously misunderstood. It comes from the Greek word *charis* which simply means a favour, a gift or a grace. When we say that someone is charismatic we mean that he or she is specially gifted or favoured. Today it has the extra meaning of being gifted by the Holy Spirit.

The prophets were the charismatic people of the Old Testament. They played a vital part in the history of Israel. In fact, over one third of the whole Old Testament is made up of prophecy. And most of that is written down in what we today would call poetic form.

About the year 1035 B.C. the political life of the Israelites underwent a major change. Up to that time, during their wanderings in the Negev desert, and later when they had settled in the land of Canaan, they had not had rulers in the strict sense of the word. They did have leaders, Moses and the other patriarchs. But these men had led the people as equals – they were of the people. A very basic idea in the whole social life of the Israelites was that they would have no other king than God himself. This seems to be enshrined in the very words of the Covenant: 'I will be your God and you will be my people'.

But now Israel had settled down. Instead of being wanderers in the desert wastes, they had become farmers in Canaan. Now, if they were to survive as a nation, they would have to deal in a business-like way with the surrounding nations. And they all had kings of their own. This change of outlook came about in the eleventh century B.C., at the time of Samuel, the last of the great local leaders who were called the Judges.

In the First Book of Samuel, you will find an account of how

Samuel bargained with God to allow the people to have a king of their own, other than God himself.

The transition was not going to be easy. They were to find that human kings were exactly that: human. Kingship was to be no guarantee against selfishness, tyranny, or even madness. However, the people wanted a monarchy, and a monarchy was set up.

The pages of the Bible begin to show us the names of the great kings, such as Saul, David and Solomon. These were men of might, power and wisdom whose names will never fade from human history. Nevertheless, the kings were a human invention and not God's idea. As long as the monarchy lasted, and it did not last long, there was to be more than a small share of trouble and tragedy.

One of the great tragedies, for a people who had been for so long close-knit and tightly bonded, was partition. In the year 935 B.C. there was a great schism. The son of King Solomon, Rehoboam, was ruling when age-old inter-tribe rivalry once more came to the boil. A combination of huge taxes and forced labour produced a rebellion. Suddenly, where there had been one kingdom, now there were two. One in the north; another, the smaller of the two, in the south. The northern kingdom called itself Israel, and the southern was called Judah, from which we get the modern name Judea.

So now there were two kingdoms, each with its own king. And for the following two centuries there were to be two parallel dynasties north and south. But, unlike the time of the great kings which we noted above, we now find a succession of men whose names have slipped away almost unnoticed: Jeroboam, Nodab Baasha and Ahab in the north, Rehoboam, Abijam Asa and Jehosophat in the south.

Although these names mean little to us, their owners did in turn set the stage for another group of men whose names meant something very important indeed, the prophets. If the kings had been the people's idea, the prophets were certainly God's, and God spoke to the kings in no uncertain terms through his prophets. They were God's spokesmen. Many books in the Bible bear their names: Isaiah, Jeremiah and Ezekiel, for example. And there were many others. The prophets lived and worked during a very long period of about four hundred years, beginning in the eighth century B.C.

Despite much misunderstanding, the foreseeing or foretelling of the future was not the main task of the prophets. They were much more concerned with shaping the future rather than foretelling it. The word 'prophet' comes from the Greek word, *phemi,* meaning 'to speak', with the prefix, *pro,* meaning 'for'. So a prophet 'speaks for' someone else. In this case that someone else was God. The prophets, first and foremost, were speakers, not writers. But they did have writers or scribes among their followers, and so their message did get preserved in written form.

What did they say, and to whom? In order to understand them and their message, we have to remember that they always spoke, first and foremost, to the people of their own generation. Sometimes their message was in words, sometimes in deeds. They proclaimed their message by their whole way of life. By their very existence they were a challenge and often a rebuke from God to his people.

Probably the greatest of the prophets was Isaiah. He was a true visionary. God revealed himself in powerful visions that left Isaiah terrified until the Spirit of God came and filled him with courage. Most of what is preserved of his message is in the form of powerful poetry. His vision and his deep religious sensibility inspired a whole school of disciples who in turn helped to keep the sense of religion alive when the people of Judah were exiles in Babylon.

The prophets were people of conviction and courage. They were powerful witnesses to God even in the face of imprisonment and death itself. Many years later, their spirit filled a man called John, on the banks of the Jordan. And his cousin. Jesus the Nazarene, was to be a new revelation of God's Word.

SIX

The Psalms

The Bible was never meant to be simply a matter of words, written or recited. Some parts of it, like the Book of Psalms, were probably composed, not even to be read aloud but to be sung during the elaborate rituals of the temple worship. Even before that, and before the development of writing, as we have seen, many of the traditions of the people, including their religious traditions, were preserved in their desert camp-fire songs.

Musical instruments are mentioned in the Bible as early as the fourth chapter of the Book of Genesis. Trumpets, flutes, harps, tambourines, cymbals and even pipe organs all feature in the pages of the Bible.

It was during the reign of King David, who was born in the year 1040 B.C., and who, in his youth, had been harpist to King Saul, that singing became organised in the worship of the Lord. The idea of a special kind of 'sacred' music probably begins with him. Under his inspiration, the music of the temple was performed by great choirs, sometimes as many as two thousand strong, chosen from the tribe of Levi, the tribe that was specially dedicated to the work of the temple.

Later, with the scattering of the people to lands where they had no temple, worship was carried out in synagogues where, again, many of the readings, blessings and psalms were set to music and celebrated in chant. The singing then, like the buildings themselves, was simpler and on a smaller scale. It became a worship-form in its own right.

One of the most quoted passages from the Bible is in the Book of Deuteronomy: 'Hear O Israel: the Lord your God is one Lord; and you shall love the Lord your God with all your heart, and with all your soul, and with all your might ... ' This is the *Shema, the* great prayer of the Jewish people. It is regularly chanted, in a variety of musical settings, in synagogue worship to this day. Jesus himself, in the twenty third chapter of Saint Matthew's Gospel, quotes it as one of the key passages of the whole Bible. It is the Great Commandment.

Similar to the chant of the synagogue is the plain chant or Gregorian chant to which the biblical texts of the Mass and the Divine Office were set during the course of many centuries in the Christian era. It has become one of the characteristics of the great European monastic tradition. The chanting of the Liturgy of the Hours is one of the mainstays of the strict monastic observance, and for centuries the stillness of the night has been broken by the gentle sound of this music, from the bare rocks of the Skellig cells to Mount Sinai itself, as monks and nuns praise their Creator in song.

While monastic communities were celebrating their liturgies through the medium of plain chant, another musical development was taking place in the great non-monastic churches and cathedrals. This was the emergence of classical polyphony, beginning in the twelfth century. Now, instead of a single melody-line, the biblical texts were set in harmony; for two, four or six sets of voices, and sometimes for as many as forty! The sixteenth century saw polyphony reach its peak in the works of such masters as Palestrina, so called after his Italian birthplace. He specialised in settings of the Mass, and his name is now often used to describe choirs devoted to the performance of his works.

A Spanish priest, very much a mystic in the style of Saint John of the Cross or Saint Teresa, was Victoria. His polyphonic settings of the texts of Holy Week, especially the words of the prophet Jeremiah, have never been surpassed.

It was during this great musical explosion of the sixteenth

century that the Reformation took place, with its stress on the use of the vernacular in worship. In England, in the years following the Reformation, the polyphonic tradition was carried on, especially in the great cathedral choir schools where the words of the vernacular liturgy were set to music. The name of William Byrd is particularly important here.

By the middle of the seventeenth century, this great productive vernacular movement had died out, but the English cathedrals and churches have preserved the fruits of that time, which might otherwise have perished in the turbulent centuries which saw the birth of the modern world.

On the far side of the Atlantic Ocean other developments were taking place. The cotton trade of the Southern States was only possible because of the development, at the same time, of the slave trade. Thousands of African slaves were shipped across the Atlantic under conditions which have themselves become part of American folklore. Those who survived the crossing were set to work in the cotton fields and at the jinmills of their white masters.

One of the things that kept their hearts up under such terrible conditions was their faith in the God of the Bible. In the biblical stories of slavery in Egypt they saw an image of their own plight. Texts and ideas from both Old and New Testaments were set to the rhythms of their work-songs. As they toiled, they sang the songs of the Exile People, and hoped, one day, for release. If none other, there was at least the promise of release through death itself. The chariot which had come to take Elijah to heaven was a symbol of this release: 'Swing low, sweet chariot, comin' for to carry me home ... ' In the Spirituals of the Southern slaves, we have not only the words but also the spirit of the Bible captured musically in a unique way.

The setting of the Bible to music is not only a thing of the past. With the renewal of the Catholic liturgy after the Second

Vatican Council, the impetus was provided once more and modern settings of the biblical texts continue to appear. The names of Deiss, Gelineau and a host of others, as yet less well known, are testimony to the revival of an ancient tradition.

It is a great pity, therefore, that the performance of the psalms (the Responsorial Psalm) at Mass is so often entrusted to the Reader. It is not her or his task. It should be done by a cantor, cantor and choir (or cantor and congregation), and where this *is* done we can experience a great enrichment of the Liturgy of the Word.

However, the fact of the matter is that, very often, it will fall to the reader to lead the congregation in the Responsorial Psalm. Once again, our attitude will be all-important. To see and understand the Book of Psalms as a collection of wonderful songs and poems in praise of God is a great help. We can take a cue from what the great Saint Ambrose had to say about the psalms:

What is more pleasing than the psalm? David himself expressed it so beautifully when he said, 'Praise the Lord! How good it is to sing psalms to our God! How pleasant to praise him!' And this is indeed true; for in the psalm there is an opportunity for the people to bless and praise God; the psalm expresses the admiration that people feel and what the people want to say; in them the Church speaks, the faith is expressed in a melodious way ... there too is heard the joyful call of freedom, the cry of pleasure and the sound of happiness. The psalm soothes anger, frees from care and drives away sadness. It is a weapon by night and a teacher by day: it is a shield in times of fear, an occasion of rejoicing for the holy, a mirror of tranquillity: it is a pledge of peace and harmony, for with the aid of the harp the psalm makes one melody from a number of different notes. The beginning of the day hears the sound of the psalm and the end of the day hears its echoes.

Reading the psalm

How is the reader to deal with the psalm? Well, first of all it is important to understand why it is there. It is intended to provide a calm period of reflection between the first two readings. The purpose of the response, therefore, is, by means of repetition, to allow one key thought to recur again and again. And that key thought will usually be one that finds echoes in one or more of the other readings. It is important to signal clearly that the psalm is a response: that's why it is desirable that there be separate readers for each reading *and* for the psalm.

Practically, should the response be announced before the psalm? Yes, and the congregation should be encouraged in their response by a glance from the reader at the end of each verse. (The practice of 'triggering' the response by the reader saying 'Response!' after each verse is aesthetically unpleasant; it breaks up the rhythm of the psalm, and is unnecessary. All that is needed is a glance.)

Occasionally the response provided will be found to be either too complicated or too long to be grasped easily by the congregation. In such a case it may be preferable to substitute another, briefer quotation from the psalm, or simply to read the psalm continuously without any response at all.

The tradition goes on

Outside the field of the liturgy, popular musical settings of the Bible have become a new trend. The haunting melodies of *Fiddler on the Roof* brought the music of the synagogue as a revelation to many a Gentile audience. *Godspell* and *Jesus Christ Superstar* have, as their inspiration, the Gospels themselves. How many people who whistle their way through the tunes of *Joseph and his Amazing Technicolour Dreamcoat* even spare a single thought for the Hebrew scribes in distant Babylon, six hundred years before the birth of Christ, without whose painstaking work the story of Joseph in Egypt might never have reached them?

SEVEN

Between the Testaments

The last section of the Old Testament to be written, the Book of Wisdom, was probably written about the year 70 B.C. After that there is a gap of about one hundred and twenty years before a man called Paul wrote a letter to some friends in a place called Thessalonica. That letter was written about the year 51 A.D., and is probably the first piece of the New Testament to have been written.

In the years between there was, nevertheless, quite an amount of literary activity. Some writings from those years were only discovered in 1947 and their finding triggered off one of the most extraordinary and exciting treasure hunts ever.

During the summer of that year a young Bedouin shepherd named Mahummad Adh-dhih, whose name means Mahummad the Wolf, was tending his goats in the desert territory close to the shore of the Dead Sea. He realised that one of his goats had disappeared. Climbing up the mountain-side in search of it, he came upon a cave entrance in the rocky surface of the cliff. He threw a stone into the cave and heard the sound of breaking crockery. Frightened, he ran away and did not return until the following day, when he brought a young cousin with him for support. When their eyes had become accustomed to the gloom of the cave they saw that there were some earthenware jars standing against the wall. It was one of these that Mahummad's stone had broken. The first two jars they inspected were empty. But in the third they found a tightly wound leather scroll. They took the scroll from the jar and brought it home.

What the two youngsters had found was the first of what the

world has come to know as the Dead Sea Scrolls. Seven scrolls in all were found at that time. Further exploration in the 1950s unearthed literally thousands of fragments of other scrolls hidden away in similar jars in dozens of caves in the same area. The immediate question was: Where did they come from? Why had this veritable library of documents been stored away in these remote caves on the banks of the Dead Sea where, barring accidents, they would never have been seen by human eyes again?

The answer lay a short distance away on the shore of the Dead Sea itself. Here there was a small group of ruins which had been known for a long time but which had not been considered terribly important. Now people began to take a new look at them and excavations were begun. What emerged were the ruins of quite an extensive Jewish settlement. It seemed to have all the characteristics of a monastery: cells, meeting rooms and a large hall which was furnished with a long plaster-topped table on which were sunk a number of ink-wells. The scientists making the excavation actually found the remains of ink in these ink-wells and this together with the discovery of further jars of the kind found in the caves established the link between the monastery and the scrolls. Meanwhile, a further group of experts was working on the problem of unrolling the two-thousand year old parchments, and having them opened out and deciphered without their falling to pieces. Most of the scrolls turned out to be copies of the books of the Old Testament. But among them was one non-scriptural scroll which gave the rules of the community that had lived in the monastery. They were a Jewish sect living a life dedicated to the study and copying out of the Scriptures. The sect were known as the Essenes.

Close beside the excavated monastery they also found a graveyard containing the mortal remains of community members. What seems to have happened was this: The Qumran

Community, as they have come to be known received a warning that the army of the Roman Empire imposing the rule of the emperor by force of arms had wiped out the Zealot resistance movement in Samaria and Judea. The same fate seemed to await Qumran as a centre of Jewish religion and culture. The community therefore packed their entire library of precious scrolls into earthenware jars and hid them in the caves of the nearby hills. Then in the year 68 A.D. the army struck and wiped out the Qumran community. Their library lay where it had been hidden until the middle of the twentieth century. And if it had not been for that stray goat ...

The last years of the Qumran community ran from 70 B.C. to 51 A.D., and during that time there was a period of three years in which a certain carpenter from Nazareth began to preach first in the lakeside towns of Galilee and later in Samaria and in Jerusalem. His message was of a new kingdom. Apart from one or two very brief references to him in the secular histories of the time, the only things known about him were what came to be written down many years after he had died. Joshua Ben Joseph or Jesus of Nazareth apparently never wrote a word. Or perhaps he wrote messages and notes. But he never wrote a book. His message was delivered by word of mouth and his instructions were that this was how it was to be done from generation to generation.

This man, of about thirty years of age, who spent no more than three years in public life, turns out to be the key figure not only of the New Testament, but also, in a very special way, of the Old Testament too. And so it was that at the same time as the community of Qumran was coming to an end a new community was beginning to form in Jerusalem itself. This was the group of followers of the Nazarene. They were led, eventually, by a group of twelve. They were held together by a bond of love for one another and for the Nazarene, who they came to be-

lieve, was still among them and whose presence they celebrated In the breaking of bread. It was among such small
groups of worshippers coming together in Palestine, Turkey,
Greece and Rome for the celebration of the Eucharist, that the
seeds of the New Testament were sown.

Jesus and the Dead Sea Scrolls

Some of the language used by John the Baptist in his preaching,
and some of the ideas contained in the teaching of Jesus himself, seem to have been foreshadowed in the teaching and language of the Qumran community, as evidenced in the Dead Sea
Scrolls. Nevertheless, it would be to stretch the findings of
archaelogists and other scholars too far to suggest, as some recent writings have, that the Scrolls were written *after* the time
of Jesus, thus reflecting some of his teachings.

On the other hand, it is by no means beyond the bounds of
possibility that either John or Jesus, or even both of them, may
have been aware of the teachings of the Essenes and, indeed,
may even have visited the Qumran community at some time.
The monastery was, after all, in that area which the Bible desig-
nates as 'the Wilderness' and both John and Jesus used to retire
to the wilderness for periods of prayer and reflection.

EIGHT

Paul

The life of Saul of Tarsus is as full of adventure as any school-boy's yarn. A dramatic kind of person himself, dramatic things tended to happen to him. He was in turn both hunter and hunted. He survived at least one attempt on his life and one shipwreck. He was mistrusted by friends and foes alike, and his writings have been, to say the least, controversial throughout the history of the Church.

Saul never met Jesus. He was only eighteen years of age at the time of the crucifixion. Yet he was so affected by one mysterious event which, he tells us, brought him face-to-face with the risen Christ, that his whole life was changed. So much followed from this that Saul, or Paul (the Christian form of his name) came to write as much as one fifth of the entire New Testament. These are the letters which he wrote to many groups of Christians throughout the Middle East, mainly in those lands which today we call Turkey and Greece.

Paul has tended to hit the headlines in recent times for his alleged male chauvinism. He certainly has some stern things to say, particularly about women's place in the Church, as he sees it. But if we were merely to write him off on the basis of a few difficult passages, we would do him an enormous injustice. Someone once said that, compared to the achievements of Paul, the doings of Alexander the Great and Napoleon pale into insignificance. In other words, perhaps there is more to Saint Paul than a few selectively chosen passages and controversial quotations might suggest.

Saul was born in Tarsus, in present-day Turkey, between the years 5 and 15 A.D. His parents were Jewish, and Paul was to appeal to his hundred-per-cent Jewish blood later in life when preaching and writing to fellow Jews. But Tarsus was a Roman city. It was part of the new Roman Empire set up around the coast of the Mediterranean Sea.

Saul's education was sophisticated. It contained elements of both Greek and Roman civilisation as well as the intensely and jealously preserved traditions of the Jewish community at Tarsus.

The young Saul was a bright boy. He underwent training to be a rabbi, that is, an expert in the sacred Scriptures. His task would be, one day, to instruct his own band of young followers in the religion of their ancestors. This early training in the Jewish Scriptures, specially in the Torah (the first five books of the Bible), was to be invaluable to him when he became a writer and preacher.

His studies brought him to Jerusalem some time in the thirties, shortly after the execution of the Galilean who had been disposed of because of his unorthodox teaching and his challenging views. At Jerusalem, Saul studied the Scriptures under the celebrated master, Gamaliel. He so immersed himself in the Law that within three years he himself had become one of the strictest of the Pharisees.

The Pharisees were a sect within Judaism. Religion for them was a matter of the strictest observance of every jot and tittle of the Law. For them, religion was law. This left little room for love as an over-riding principle. That was one reason why they had been so opposed to the teachings of the Galilean, who had seemed to be talking mostly about love at the expense of the strict observance of the Law. It was this group of hard-liners that Saul joined in Jerusalem.

Then he came to hear about the followers of the executed Jesus of Nazareth, who were claiming that Jesus was not dead at all. They were not content to worship in the synagogues, but even interrupted the service and gave sermons about Jesus. Not only that, but they also held unofficial prayer-meetings in their homes.

All this was too much for Saul. These people were not keeping the rules. They were traitors, and would have to be put down. Saul was a man of action. He got letters of authority from the synagogue and set up a search-and-destroy operation against the followers of the Nazarene. As he set off on this mission, something happened to him that was to change not only his life but which was to have its effect on every generation of Christians since. In the book known as the Acts of the Apostles, which immediately follows the Gospels in our New Testament, there are no fewer than three accounts of what happened. He was struck from his horse, blinded, and he heard the Lord Jesus talking to him. It was the beginning of a complete change in Paul's life. The enthusiasm with which he had set out to destroy the Christians was now harnessed to the Church. He began a life completely devoted to the spread of the Gospel that he had once hoped to obliterate.

After that came three years during which we have very little idea of what happened to Paul. He seems to have gone off into the desert, on a kind of retreat, possibly in one of the monastic communities like that at Qumran.

When he came back from the desert, his first attempts to preach were pretty dismal. The Christians did not trust him. After all, he had been a notorious persecutor of the Church. His fellow Jews and Pharisees were out for his blood. To them he was a turncoat, a renegade. On one occasion he had to be smuggled out of Damascus in a laundry basket to save his life.

But soon there was a change of fortune. Paul was discovered by a Christian called Barnabas who introduced him to his fellow Christians. With Barnabas, Paul developed a new kind of project. They would become missionaries, taking the word of

Jesus out of the Jewish world and into the Gentile world of the Roman Empire. Setting out, they went first to Cyprus and then to a whole series of cities and towns in what is now Turkey. Their journeys are described in Acts, chapters 13 and 14.

On their travels they got mixed receptions. Sometimes, to their embarrassment, they were treated almost as gods. At other times they were stoned and left for dead. But every place they visited, they left behind them a little group of converts. These groups became the new Churches.

After Paul had left their cities, people had begun to say that you could not be a follower of Jesus unless you became a Jew first. The Gentiles became confused. Did they have to accept circumcision and conform to the Law of Moses before they could be baptized as Christians? Paul did the only possible thing at short notice. He dashed off a letter to the Churches he had set up in Galatia, telling them to accept no other version of the Gospel except what he had preached to them.

Thus, two things have now happened which will continue to be characteristic of the life of Paul: travel and writing. Travel was essential if the good news of the Gospel was to spread. Letters were essential if the newly founded Churches were to be kept in touch and abreast of developments.

And so, in Saint Paul's letters you will find extensive treatment of the basics: Baptism, faith, law, original sin, Jesus Christ crucified and risen, and indeed, love itself. Paul wrote about love on dozens of occasions. Look at Chapter 13 of his first letter to the Church at Corinth for a classic of Christian writing.

Because Paul was writing long before any of the Gospels were written, it is not surprising that we find the first-ever account of the celebration of the Eucharist in one of his letters. It is found in his first letter to the Christians of the Greek city of Corinth, and is probably basically a description of how the Eucharist was celebrated in the city of Corinth (1 Corinthians 11:23-24).

Throughout the centuries, praise and blame have been heaped on Paul's head. There has rarely been a great movement within Christianity for which authority has not been claimed from the writings of Saint Paul.

Tradition tells us that he died a martyr's death in Rome after a long period of house-arrest in that city. He died the privileged death of a Roman citizen (if beheading can be called a privilege; at least it was quicker than crucifixion!). His execution probably took place in the year 67.

Paul, the man who brought the young Church into contact with the Roman empire, was now dead. But he left behind him a collection of letters as valuable, in their own way, as anything else within the covers of the Bible. They are the earliest written accounts of the Christian message.

The Reader and Paul

Paul wrote letters as we write letters: sometimes to individual friends or colleagues, and at other times to groups – normally his converts in one town or another. But whether addressed to an individual or a group, today we read his letters *as a Church*, knowing that the message is both personal and general.

To be faithful to Paul and his intention, we ought to be able to judge the appropriate tone of the letter. A letter of praise will sound different from a letter of blame. But the directness of a letter never changes: it is an intimate form of communication, not like a notice or an announcement.

Paul often has multiple motivations – to instruct, to console, to encourage, upbraid, warn or intercede. Know what he is trying to accomplish.

Go slowly with the letters. Paul can be complex, changing mood and intention, sometimes even within a single paragraph. Try to love those who hear you as Paul loved those to whom he wrote.

NINE

Three Gospels

'Gospel' is a word that means, simply 'Good News'. The Good News in question is the news of salvation. In the Bible, four books are given the description Gospel, each one attributed to one of the four Evangelists, Matthew. Mark, Luke and John.

Taken together, the four Gospels are the high point of the New Testament writings and, indeed, of the whole Bible. They are all relatively short books, and each has its own enigmatic contribution to make. Although they were quite clearly written by four different people, they have one thing above all in common: they all tell about the life and death of the same central character.

This Joshua Ben Joseph certainly was a real historical person. His birth is described and an indication is even given of the time of his birth. In those days there seems to have been a continuous process of head-counting going on in the Roman Empire. It probably had to do with the collection of taxes. The birth of Jesus is located in time just as one of these censuses was taking place. The account of his young life, however, is only of the scantiest. He seems to have grown up and been educated in his home town of Nazareth, from where he moved north and made his adult home on the banks of the Sea of Galilee.

At the age of about thirty, he begins to preach publicly about a new Kingdom to be established. He stresses that this is not something new at all, but rather it is based firmly on the old Jewish Scriptures. 'Think not that I have come to abolish the Law and the Prophets; I have come not to abolish them, but to fulfil them,' he said. This is the very centre of the preaching of Jesus, no matter which of the four Gospels you pick up. He insisted that all people are sisters and brothers, a concept based, in turn, on his teaching about the fatherhood of God. This meant that there were to be no barriers. Everybody must be acceptable to everyone else, Jew or Gentile, rich or poor, Israelite or Roman. The problem was not that he preached these doctrines, but that, embarrassingly, he practised what he preached, and expected others to do the same.

He tended to mix with the 'wrong' people. Self-respecting Jews would have nothing to do with public sinners, Samaritans, members of the Roman occupation force, or with anyone who collaborated with it, like Matthew, who collected taxes to finance the occupation. But these were precisely the type of people that Jesus insisted on talking to and helping. Such behaviour was relatively unimportant as long as it was confined to the small town on the Sea of Galilee. It was another matter entirely when Jesus came south to Jerusalem. One day, seated on the colt of an ass, cheered at first by a handful of children, but later merging into the crowds in the narrow streets, he rode into trouble.

It might have been alright out in the country to insist that all people are brothers and sisters. But to bring such thinking into the corridors of power and privilege, and even into the court-yard of the temple itself – this was going too far. In the shadows, beneath the sleepy domed roofs, there were those who saw him as a threat. A friend was bribed. A trap was set ... and sprung. A show trial was arranged, and the Nazarene was sentenced to death, which was, as we now know, anything but the end of the story.

Considering the importance of what he did and what he taught, it seems extraordinary to us that Jesus of Nazareth apparently never wrote a word. In fact he probably wrote as much as any other ordinary person did in those days, which was not a lot. But he certainly never wrote anything like a Gospel, or even an Epistle. This fact is, in itself, very important for us when we come to examine what kind of writings the Gospels are. It is most important to realise that between the crucifixion and the appearance of the first Gospel there was a gap of twenty or thirty years.

The first problem facing the preachers or writers of the Good News about Jesus was to explain the crucifixion. How could such an apparent failure be shown to be a success? Their method was to show that the crucifixion fulfilled the prophecies of the Old Testament. They went on from there to stress that this Jesus, who had indeed been put to death, was, nevertheless, now risen from the dead. They had met him, and the person they had met after the crucifixion was the very same person whom they had met, worked with and lived with on the shores of the Sea of Galilee. In other words, it was a question of identification: this was the self-same Jesus. Further, we find in these accounts their teaching on the consequences of the crucifixion and subsequent resurrection, namely, that people should repent of their sins and be baptized in the name of the same Lord Jesus.

That was the shape of the apostolic teaching as echoed in the writings of Matthew, Mark and Luke. John was somewhat different and we shall look at him in the next chapter. For the present let us concentrate on the other three.

Matthew was one of the twelve apostles. (Not all of the evangelists were.) Neither Mark nor Luke had been apostles nor had they known Jesus during his life on earth. Matthew, on the other hand, did know him. Matthew was a Jew, and his Gospel was probably written about the year 75 A.D. His purpose was to tell other Jewish converts about the life and teaching of Jesus. He stresses that Jesus is not only alive, but is to be found wherever two or three are gathered in his name. Some experts would say that the version of Matthew's Gospel that has come down to us is a Greek version of an older Aramaic text.

Mark's full name was John Mark. Although he was not an apostle, he is mentioned in the Acts of the Apostles. He was an associate and travelling-companion of Saint Paul. He was also a fellow preacher and interpreter of Saint Peter. It was Mark's task to gather together and set down the teachings of Saint Peter. He probably did his writing in Rome in the years between 60 and 70 A.D. Greek, and not Latin, was the most commonly spoken language in the Roman Empire at that time. Mark's readers were the Greek-speaking Jews living in Rome at that time. He also had a wider audience of non-Jews and thus he goes to great pains, in his Gospel, to explain Jewish customs and terms for them.

Saint Luke, our third evangelist, like Mark, never met Jesus. He wrote two books: his Gospel and the book which we call the Acts of the Apostles. He too wrote mainly for Gentiles who had become converted to the new faith. He, like Mark, was, for some of his life, a companion to Saint Paul; and, as in Saint Paul's writings, his main message is the message of universality: Salvation was available to all and sundry, Jew or Gentile, slave or free. All that was needed was faith in Jesus Christ, crucified and risen.

One of the most remarkable things about Luke's Gospel is the extraordinarily intimate detail in which he describes the time before the birth of our Lord, the first Christmas and other childhood incidents, framed in poetic language which beautifully echoes the prayers and expectations of the Old Testament. It would seem that he may have got his information from someone who was very close to the Holy Family at that time. There are those who claim to see here the first-hand account possibly given to him by our Lady herself.

Taken together, the Gospels of Matthew, Mark and Luke are called the Synoptic Gospels. 'Synoptic' is a Greek word which simply means that they share one point of view. They deal with much the same material and in much the same way. However, this is only partly true. Although there are many similarities they also differ in detail when dealing with the same incident, yet in other parts it is hard not to believe that they have copied passages from one another.

Perhaps a clue to the right understanding of the Gospels is to realise what a Gospel is not. A Gospel is not a straight, simple historical account of something that happened two thousand years ago. The Gospels were written by people who had faith. Before they ever wrote a word they believed that Jesus of Nazareth had risen from the dead. Their accounts of what he said and did were written in the light of that faith. The writers were people of faith, enthusiasm and hindsight. They did not write in order to convince people about the resurrection. They did not set out to convince people that Jesus was God incarnate. They presumed that the people who would read their Gospels were believers already. If we remember that the Gospels were written with hindsight, they make much more sense than if we were to see them as non-interpretative history. They were written *by* people of faith *for* people of faith.

TEN

The Fourth Gospel

The Gospel of Saint John is different from the others. It contains extra material. He tells of miracles not mentioned by the others, even one as important as the raising of Lazarus. It would seem that, while the other Gospels may have in some way grown out of a common oral tradition, that of Saint John seems to have had a different starting-point.

There is, however, quite a lot of material that is covered by the other Gospels too. And it certainly concerns itself with the same central character: Jesus of Nazareth.

As explained in the previous chapter, before a word of any of the Gospels came to be written down, there was a solid oral tradition: the faith as handed from group to group and from generation to generation. This tradition was based on the preaching of the apostles. It was out of this shared tradition that the Synoptic Gospels grew. One of the apostles who preached that message of a Jesus, crucified and risen, was the son of Zebedee, John. Traditionally, the fourth Gospel is thought to be based on his experience both as a young follower of Jesus and later as a preacher. It would seem that his Gospel, as it has come down to us is a 'second edition', possibly committed to paper by somebody else, but using the experience and the insights of John, to which extra material was added in order to deal with objections and difficulties that arose at a later date.

Many experts agree that the most likely place for the writing of the fourth Gospel was the city of Ephesus, in present-day Turkey but then part of the Greek world. There was a Christian Church there, and it has long been a popular belief that the Gospel of John was written there between the years 90 and 100

A.D. By that time John himself would have been an old man, but the view of Jesus that his Gospel gives is the view of the young John. It is coloured by John's insights into the whole wonder and mystery of Jesus, a wonder that deepened and grew during the course of his long life.

We get a glimpse of the young John in his account of what happened when he and Peter got the news of the empty tomb on the first Easter morning: John was off like a shot, sprinting to the tomb. Peter arrived, a poor, and probably breathless, second.

John has always been seen as a special friend of Jesus. He sat next to him at the Last Supper. He is often called 'the disciple whom Jesus loved' and, of course, he was the only one of the disciples with the courage to remain on Calvary to the very end. The final act of friendship came when Jesus himself asked him to take care of his mother.

Clearly, there is a very intimate source for the information that we find in the pages of the fourth Gospel. Experts divide the book into two parts: the Book of Signs, and the Book of Glory. *Sign* is John's word for what others term a miracle. The first part of his Gospel, the Book of Signs, is built around the narrative of several miracles. Two of these took place in one spot, the little town of Cana. There he worked his first sign, the changing of water into wine at the wedding feast. There too he spoke with the official whose son was ill unto death at Capernaum. Jesus heard his entreaty and cured his child. Jesus may have had a soft spot for Cana. Perhaps he had friends or relations there. Whatever the reason, the people of Cana were twice witness to signs of divine generosity.

Generosity was something that we find Jesus using as a 'teaching aid' again and again. John's description of the Multiplication of the Loaves and Fishes is a prime example. To understand what John was getting at in telling of such events we have to realise that he was writing from a deep knowledge of the Old Testament where, again and again, it was pointed out that the coming of the New Kingdom would be marked by signs of great abundance: signs of God's generosity. But that is not all. John straight away goes on to link this particular sign with that other altogether greater gift, the Eucharist. It would be helpful at this stage to read through the whole of Chapter Six of Saint John's Gospel. It is a masterpiece of teaching.

Immediately linked to the notion of the Eucharist is another key idea in Saint John: the idea of giving life. The idea of life and life-giving is one of the most prominent recurring ideas in all of the Fourth Gospel. Someone has calculated that *life* and *life-giving* are mentioned a total of fifty four times in this one Gospel. In fact, looking at it one way, the whole of this Gospel is about life and the fact that Jesus is the Lord of Life. In the eleventh chapter, where he tells of the raising of Lazarus, John constantly stresses not just the wonder of the event but its significance for us in understanding Jesus as master of life and death.

The second part of John's Gospel, the Book of Glory, really begins with Chapter Thirteen. This is his account of the Last Supper. It is no mere description of a meal. Nor is it just an account of the institution of the Eucharist. Saint John uses it as an opportunity to build in a long and detailed summary of the teaching of Jesus on the Eucharist, the Father, and prayer. This is followed by John's account of the passion and death of Jesus.

Here again, it is not difficult to see the difference between John and the other evangelists. The Synoptics show us the body of Jesus, broken, on the cross. It bears all the signs of the sufferings he has been through. His agony is reflected in the faces of the crowd. This is the place of the Skull. The scene is a tortured one. The sky is dark and there is an atmosphere of foreboding everywhere.

But with John it is different. He sees the death of Jesus in the light of what Jesus himself had said at the Last Supper and in the garden. This is not the tortured death of a falsely-accused victim. This is the death of the Lord of Life, the man who said that no one could take his life from him unless he laid it down himself. This is the death of the man who proclaimed his death as a sign of the glory of the Father.

In John's account of the crucifixion, and in the chapters that follow it, the glory of the Father is already breaking through. It is no longer a matter of a death. It is rather a question of death-and-resurrection. John himself said: 'We had seen his glory; the glory of God the Father'.

And this brings us to the beginning. Most good books have a preface, and the preface is usually written when the rest of the book has been completed. This is true of Saint John's Gospel too. The opening pages of the book are a preface in which is summed up everything in the pages that follow. In his very first few sentences John tries to hint at what lies in store. He gives us a glimpse of God the Creator, of eternity, of the mystery of the incarnation and what it means for humankind. 'In the beginning was the Word ... and the Word was made flesh ... '

ELEVEN

The sources

Like Baptism and the Eucharist, the Bible is one of those things which the divided Churches hold in common. Whatever divisions have marred the two thousand years of Church history, the Bible has been revered by all. For all, it has been both a source book and a prayer book. Ecumenical study of the Scriptures, therefore, has been one of the very highly valued developments of recent years. An Irish inter-church working party made a valuable report on Church, Scripture and Authority. What follows is a summary of their findings.

While the works of creation manifest the goodness, wisdom and power of God, nevertheless, in his eternal love, and amid the disorder created by the sins of humankind, he chose to reveal himself and to make known to us the hidden purpose of his saving will in the history of a people. This plan of salvation was realised in deeds and words. 'In many and various ways, God spoke of old to our fathers by the prophets. But in these last days he has spoken to us by a son' (Hebrews 1:1-2). The revelation has come to us supremely through Christ, the Word made flesh, 'full of grace and truth' (John 1:14).

The ministry of Jesus has been one of reconciliation, 'for in him all the fullness of God was pleased to dwell, and through him to reconcile all things to himself, whether on earth or in heaven, making peace by the blood of his cross' (Colossians 1:19-20). Christ continues this living ministry through his Church.

The books of the Old and the New Testaments testify to God's saving acts for all humankind. It is within the people chosen as his own that the Scriptures take their origin. They are the written record of his saving plan, which comes to completion in Christ and his people. We recognise that the Scriptures are the Word of God because they are inspired by his Holy Spirit.

Authority in the Church arises out of its nature and task. Each Church would accept that there exists some kind of authority, which extends at least to the interpretation of Scripture. This authority must always be based on the authority of Christ which is that of both servant and shepherd.

In the Roman Catholic Church, authority resides in the pope as an individual in virtue of his office, or in the pope and the bishops in communion with him acting collegially.

Within the framework of a final appeal to 'God's Word Written' the Anglican Communion would see the bishops as guardians of the faith.

The General Assembly of the Presbyterian Church would be the Presbyterians' interpreter of the Word of God in Scripture, under the guidance of the Holy Spirit, the Westminster Confession of Faith being regarded as a subordinate standard.

The Lutheran Church, in matters of doctrine, would look to the Church leaders (bishops) with the counsel of theologians.

The Methodist Church would speak of Church teaching in less formal and in more inspirational terms. Final decisions would lie, after full dialogue, with the Conference.

In the sixteenth century, the divine origin and inspiration of the Scriptures were generally recognised. The real problem arose as to whether the Scriptures *alone* were sufficient of themselves for salvation. Nor could agreement be reached as to whether the Scriptures spoke with clarity without the assistance of the Church. From the sixteenth century to the present day much scholarly research has taken place, and a simple identification of Scripture with Revelation is not generally supposed. It is now more adequately recognised that tradition and

Scripture intertwine, both in the formulation of Scripture and its place within the Church.

How then do the Churches differ in their view of the relation between Scripture, tradition and the teaching authority of the Church?

Roman Catholic

The Roman Catholic view of Revelation is as follow. In his goodness and wisdom God chose to reveal himself to us. Having spoken in many places and in various ways, last of all he has spoken to us by his Son. Jesus does not only speak about God: he is himself the Word of God. Jesus is God's revelation not only in his teaching but in himself. Add to this the notion of tradition. The Second Vatican Council said: 'What was handed on by the apostles includes everything that contributes to the holiness of life and the increase in faith of the People of God. And so, the Church, in her teaching, life and worship perpetuates and hands on to all generations all that she herself is, all that she believes' (*Constitution on Revelation*, 8).

It is on the precise question of determining what is and what is not authentic tradition that the Churches are divided. Deeply ingrained in the Reformed tradition is a strong suspicion of any suggestion that the Church is constantly moving towards the fullness of the truth. Christianity recognises only one absolute authority, God himself. His word is mediated to us by a delicately balanced system embracing Scripture, tradition and the teaching authority. None of these is absolute in the sense that God's word alone is absolute. Sacred Scripture is not simply the Word of God but the privileged witness to that Word. An absolute identification of the Scriptures and the Word of God, as the biblical fundamentalist might conceive it, can hardly claim support in the Bible itself or in the theology of the Reformers. The Bible is always read in the light of tradition.

'It is clear therefore that sacred tradition, sacred Scripture and the teaching authority of the Church, in accord with God's most wise design, are so linked and joined together, and each in its own way, under the action of the Holy Spirit, contribute effectively to the salvation of souls' (Vatican II, *Constitution on Revelation*, 10).

Anglican

Churches of the Anglican Communion would say that the Scriptures are sufficient as a repository of the truth. 'Holy Scripture containeth all things necessary to salvation: so that whatsoever is not read therein, nor may be proved thereby, is not to be required of any man, that it should be believed as an article of the faith, or be thought requisite necessary to salvation' (*Articles of Religion*, VI)

In hearing and reading, in teaching and expounding the Scriptures, the Church witnesses to their truth and passes on from age to age the faith once for all delivered to the saints. The Holy Spirit who spoke through the prophets, interprets the Scriptures in the life of the Church. Thus the Church is a witness to and keeper of the Scriptures. Thus the Church has attached great importance to tradition, not as an alternative to Scripture, but as a means to its correct interpretation.

Scripture interpreted by the Church is the norm or standard of the Christian faith. Tradition brings out the meaning of Scripture and testifies to the Scripture as the supreme standard to which it must conform and by which it is assessed.

Presbyterian

The Presbyterians would say that God has revealed himself specially to the people chosen to receive his salvation, to whom his eternal Son came as a man for the salvation of humankind. This unique revelation, through which God continues to teach his Church, is to be found in the Old Testament and in the New.

This revelation is handed down in the Church, 'traditioned', as Saint Paul says about the account of the Lord's Supper or the resurrection, or what he taught the Thessalonians. This is therefore the basic tradition. Through the guidance of the Holy Spirit its significance is made clear in the Church through the witness of the Church's teachers and members, who always remain servants of the revealed Word of God.

Thus there is the basic tradition enshrined in Scripture. This and its interpretation are handed down in the Church; and the interpretation of the basic tradition and the checking of the (other) traditions which grow out of it have constantly to be done as the Spirit of God guides his Church. The Church has authority as well as responsibility to decide on these matters, but this authority itself must be constantly subjected to the basic revelation and is not necessarily free from error.

Methodists

Methodists would say that the Holy Scriptures are the inspired witness to the revelation of God, and constitute the supreme rule of faith. The Bible is unique because that to which it bears witness is unique, unrepeatable, sufficient – the divine revelation in Jesus Christ. The Church has not made up its Gospel from its own experience, but has received it from witnesses, and the Holy Spirit assures us that their witness is true. That sacred history to which the Scriptures witness, constitutes the terms of reference for the whole life and action of the Church until the end of time.

The fact that the Christian faith rests on a series of historical events interpreted as the very work of God in the world 'for us and for our salvation', and that we live in an historical period different from and later than the events themselves, makes tradition in the sense of the 'traditioning' process and in the sense of the handing down of the faith from one generation to another, both inevitable and inescapable.

The principle, therefore, that the Church, at all stages of its history, seeks to reform itself under the Word of God, is an essential principle of its life.

Scripture and tradition need not be put over and against one another. Behind both is the living Word of God, the Word made flesh in Jesus Christ. The continuing flow of Christian existence from one generation to another would not have been possible apart from the presence and work of the Holy Spirit.

Conclusion

The report of the Working Party concludes by saying:

'We have recalled with thankfulness how much we hold in common as Christians, in that we all invoke the True God and confess Jesus as Lord and Saviour. We accept that in our times a fuller understanding of what divides us would seem, under God's grace, to be revealing patterns of convergence and these have certainly led to a greater longing for unity.

'We frankly recognise that in certain important matters our convictions still differ. However, even where there are differences reaching beyond questions of emphasis to belief itself, our experience in meeting one another as friends and brothers in Christ has led us to increased respect for and understanding of one another and the quality of Christian life in our separated communions'.

References

The Inter-Church Report on 'Church, Scripture and Authority' is published in Cahal Daly and Stanley Worrall (editors) *Ballymascanlon: An Adventure in Inter-Church Dialogue*, Belfast. Christian Journals Ltd, Dublin, Veritas, 1978.

The Constitution on Revelation is available in Austin Flannery OP (editor) *Vatican Council II: Conciliar and Post-Conciliar Documents*, Dublin, Dominican Publications. 1992 edition.

TWELVE

Biblical truth

Jesus told Pilate, 'I have come into the world to bear witness to the truth. Everyone who is of the truth hears my voice'. And Pilate said to him, 'What is truth?' Or, to paraphrase, How true is true? How true is the Bible, our lectionary for us? Has the Bible anything to say to the late twentieth century?

Start with the Old Testament. Here is a whole collection of books that are packed with the extraordinary. That is not too surprising. Things that are *ordinary* hardly become history, to be handed down across the generations. The same is true today. The ordinary does not sell newspapers, or get into the t.v. news. It is the extraordinary things that get noticed, that get talked about. It was no different in the past. The Bible is the record of the extraordinary. Books full of wonder.

Moses crossed the desert to the burning bush and to his first meeting with Yahweh because he was puzzled. He wondered why the bush was not consumed by the flames. That was the day on which God revealed himself, and his name, to a human. God, by revealing himself to humankind, in a certain sense hands himself over to us. The wonder of the burning bush was nothing to the wonder which Moses and his people felt when they realised what it meant to enter a relationship with almighty God. No matter how unfaithful they may have been to his covenant from time to time, they never ceased to feel a sense of awe at the thought that God had revealed himself, and in a sense entrusted himself to their care.

From then on, as far as the Hebrews were concerned, their world-view always involved an interweaving of the supernatural with the natural. Even natural events, thunderstorms or hailstones, were seen, understood and interpreted as signs of that Creator who stood behind all reality.

The one thing that will stop a desert being a desert is water. Water will turn the desert sand into a fertile garden. When they were wandering in the desert, in response to God's invitation, and when water was suddenly provided for them, the Hebrews recognised in this a sign of the God who cared for them. It did not really matter whether there may have been a perfectly plausible, natural reason for the arrival of the water. As far as they were concerned, this was God's doing.

Today, vast areas of what was desert in the time of Moses is fertile farmland. World-wide resources and modern agricultural machinery have combined to change the desert into fertile land. Is that any less of a wonder now, even if we do understand a bit more about how things work?

The greatest wonder of the Old Testament was the escape from Egypt. A group of people (probably not quite the vast horde of the Hollywood version!) left the Egypt of Rameses II and escaped across the Red Sea onto the Sinai peninsula. This was the Exodus, the deliverance for which the Jewish people have given thanks ever since. Does it really matter that our knowledge of the climate of this area now shows it to be perfectly possible that the Hebrews crossed the Red Sea where it is narrowest and shallowest during one of the seasons when the hot wind from the desert actually dries up the muddy sea bed and allows passage in comparative safety? The fact of such conditions is simply there. The dramatic darkness and the walls of water to right and left, which the Bible speaks of, may well be the totally legitimate embellishments of a great event that passed into folklore. And that folklore is based on a faith in a Creator and a protecting God. It was the ability to recognise God behind the events of nature that was part of the faith of Moses and his people.

And what of us today? Do we have a choice? Does a deeper understanding of the world we live in mean that we must reject the idea of a Creator? Is the biblical understanding of the world completely opposed to a present-day, scientific understanding of the same world?

Scientist and mathematician, Stephen Hawking, who would not claim to be particularly religious, but who is widely regarded as the most brilliant theoretical physicist since Einstein, says: 'If we find the answer [to the question, Why is it that we and the universe exist?] it would be the ultimate triumph of human reason – for then we would know the mind of God.' (*A Brief History of Time*, 1988, p. 185)

The New Testament, in turn, presents us with a new kind of wonder, particularly in the miracles of Jesus himself. It is certainly very important to understand these miracles. What in fact did Jesus do? And what did he hope to achieve by performing them? After all, anybody can work a miracle if a miracle is no more than a particularly clever conjuring trick. The best of conjuring tricks will not convince you that the magician is a new messiah, much less that he is a god! We have seen too many conjuring tricks to be taken in by them. We know that anyone who knows the secret, or is a member of the Magic Circle, can 'change' water into wine. But the Gospels simply do not show Jesus, or the apostles for that matter, as tricksters. And there were certainly tricksters around in those days. Whenever Jesus did one of his 'signs', we have got to be sure not only of what he did, but also of why he did it. His purpose was never to bamboozle people into believing in him. He never performed a miracle to force people's faith. But he gave signs to confirm faith when it was already there.

The miracles of Jesus have always been a problem. (If they could be explained away they would hardly be miracles!) Some people have tended to write them off altogether. This hardly

seems reasonable in the face of the massive amount of testimony to them. Some have said that miracles are simply impos-
sible, therefore did not happen, therefore were the inventions
of the evangelists.

But, nevertheless, it does seem that Jesus did, in fact, cure
people and exorcise them. Calling these wonders by another
name would not seem to solve the problem. To insist that Jesus
could not have done miracles would be to trap God in his own
creation. If he is truly Lord of creation, then creation is his to
control. Nevertheless, on the other hand, to demand that God
should constantly intervene to frustrate the laws of his own
creation would seem to be equally unreasonable.

Jesus, of course, did not always perform the miracles that
people demanded of him. 'This generation seeks a sign. But no
sign will be given to it ... ' Signs simply do not work for people
who do not understand them. Signs do not speak to non-be-
lievers. The musical show *Jesus Christ, Superstar* has Herod taunt
Jesus: 'Prove to me that you're no fool, walk across my swim-
ming pool'. But it was not the time for a conjuring trick. Conjuring tricks are not worthy of the message of either the New or
the Old Testaments.

Something much more extraordinary and much more wonderful is involved. It is the personal involvement of God with
us, and us with God. That is the message, not just of the miracles, but of every page of the Bible and of our lectionary.

THIRTEEN

Getting it right

As we said at the very beginning, what we are dealing with, above all, as readers, is meaning. There is a meaning in every page we read. That meaning has got to be delivered to those who will hear us read. And it is highly unlikely that any reading will make sense to our hearers if it does not make sense to us first.

Every page of Scripture had an original author. That author wrote what he wrote so that his message would be available to others. Therefore it follows that we must first of all discover what his purpose was. When we have found that we may well know what has to be conveyed to our Sunday congregation.

On the other hand, there may, on occasion, be further layers of meaning or implication, originally unsuspected, but which God the Holy Spirit has for today's listeners. Hence the need for both prayer and study in our preparation for each Sunday.

It can also be the case that there may be several points in a single reading, one of which may need stressing on a particular day because it corresponds with something in one of the other readings or, indeed, with a point to be stressed by that day's preacher. None of this works by intuition. Discussion and consultation are an essential part of preparation.

When we are sure that we understand the message, then our task is to determine how that message is best conveyed. It should go without saying that the faith-based interest and even enthusiasm of the reader for his or her message will be felt by the listeners. So will boredom or lack of interest!

Using emphasis

Our meaning will be conveyed by the way we handle our material; the colour we give our sentences and phrases; the way, above all, that we handle emphasis.

Emphasis can be given to a word or phrase by a change in volume, or by a change in speed, or even by a simple pause. The decision as to which to use, and where to use it, will have been made at the preparation stage; not during the actual reading. A discreet pencil-mark might even be a help. (If writing in the margin of a lectionary or desk Bible, be sure that it is done by agreement and with a *soft* lead pencil. Then there is little chance of damage to the page and it will be easily erased later.)

Being prepared and at ease

When it comes to the day itself, nothing should be left to the last minute. By arriving early we are able not just to compose ourselves in prayer, but also to 'check the ground'. This means making sure that the lectionary is in place (if it is not to be carried in procession), and that the marker ribbons are where they should be.

There will also be time to re-check the day's message and emphasis with other readers and with the celebrant. And finally there are the amplifier settings. We will have more to say about sound systems below. Suffice it here to say that beforehand is the time to make sure that the system is switched on, live and correctly set. To treat a congregation to the thump of a tapped microphone or the crack of a thrown switch is a kind of assault, and will certainly play havoc with a prayerful atmosphere.

For the liturgy itself, one of our most valuable assets will be composure. This in turn is generated by the self-confidence that comes from good preparation. Our bearing will reflect the seriousness with which we approach the task of dealing with God's Word. At the appropriate time we will approach the lectern without rushing, open the lectionary, check once more that the page is correct (if it is not, no need to panic. Simply take your time and open it at the correct one. You will have checked the page number before Mass!), establish yourself comfortably and start to read.

Almost all newcomers to public reading begin by reading too fast. Nervousness is partly to blame, and that can soon be overcome. But even then, speed is a constant problem. We have constantly to check our speed, best of all by having a colleague listen to us from the back of the church and comment frankly. One reason why we tend to talk too fast is that in normal face-to-face conversation we can afford to do so; we are close to our listener and there are few distractions. In church, the situation is quite different. Some folk will be quite a distance from us, they may be surrounded by distractions of one kind or another, even the traffic noise outside, of which they may not be consciously aware.

And remember, while you are by now very familiar with your reading and with its message, because you have prepared, they may not have heard it for three years, may not be familiar with it and will have to grasp it first time round or miss it entirely! So do not spoil their chances. They cannot turn back and read a complex passage again, as you may well have done in preparation .

What about interruptions and distractions? They do happen, so it is as well to be prepared. The only thing to do about a distraction is to cope with it! It is no use pretending that it is not there. You may try to battle through, but your listeners will not be with you. A low-flying jet plane cannot be beaten. A pause, and perhaps a smile, depending on the circumstances, will be understood. Interruptions usually pass within a matter of seconds. Better to lose the seconds than to lose the message.

The self-assurance and comfort that come from good preparation mean that we will be sufficiently familiar with our text to be able to lift our eyes from the page from time to time as we read. This is important because we use our eyes as well as our voice to communicate. To meet the eyes of the congregation, even for the occasional fleeting moment, particularly if an important point is being made, is most important. It is not a question of staring; simply a matter of normal, human contact.

Using microphones

Now, a word about microphones. Or, rather, about sound systems as a whole.

For centuries there were no such things. That did not mean that readers and preachers were not heard. Just that they had to go about their task in a somewhat different, and possibly more careful, way.

If sound systems are to be a help, and sometimes they can be quite a hindrance, they have got to be properly understood. We have got to have some idea of what they can do, and what they cannot. (They cannot, for instance, un-mumble a mumble!)

The normal sound system consists of three elements: the microphone, which 'collects' the sounds which we make, and feeds them into the system; the amplifier which takes those sounds, amplifies them and feeds them on to the third element, the loudspeaker. This latter is usually in the form of a box, or enclosure, mounted on wall or pillar, to bring the sounds to the ears of the listeners.

Control of the system is usually exercised at the amplifier. Volume and frequencies (treble and bass) are all capable of control and very often need to be set differently for different voices. That is why they are there in the first place. The correct settings for different voices, congregation size and size of church can only be determined by trial, with careful noting of what settings are suitable for what conditions.

From the point of view of the reader on the job, the most important and most accessible element is the microphone and so here are a few basic rules: Never touch a mike. It should be switched on and appropriately positioned before Mass begins. Never tap or strike a live mike. As we noted before, this can be a kind of assault on our hearers. It can also seriously damage the instrument. Microphones are designed to cope with nothing more robust than changes in air-pressure (sounds). The microphone should be positioned in such a way that it points more or less directly at the mouth of the reader, but should not be so high or so close that it masks or hides the reader's face. People need to watch you as you read.

A well designed and adjusted sound system will do its job without drawing attention to itself. It will be set neither too low, in which case people will not hear anyway, or too loud, in which case it will distort and even obscure the message by drawing attention to itself and away from the reading.

Sound systems are no magic answer. They can be a blessing or a curse, depending on how they are put to work.

Using your eyes

Of course we use our eyes to read the text on the page of the lectionary. But that's not all. Use of the eyes is an important part of our task in communicating.

A head buried in the lectionary is pretty ineffectual. We have got to have the ability and the confidence to be able to look up, not just at the roof of the church or at some vague spot above the heads of the hearers. Talking convincingly to people requires looking them straight in the eye.

How often have you felt uncomfortable if someone would not look straight at you in conversation? Eye contact is a vital part of the message.

Most important is our own belief in what we are reading.

Hence the need for good study in preparation. Confidence removes fear, and confidence comes from firm belief in what we are reading.

What if our readers will not look back? Perhaps they have their heads buried too – in a missalette or prayer book. Never mind. If your bearing and your reading are confident and meaningful enough they will find they do not need their missalettes. And that is how it should be: a good reader eventually makes missalettes unnecessary.

The secret of good use of the eyes is to look up, however briefly, at the end of a sentence or paragraph, looking directly at one or another member of the congregation, varying the direction of your glance each time. In this way people will intuit that you are in some way addressing each one of them. This in turn gives a sense of personal involvement – and your reading comes to life.

FOURTEEN

Reading the Prayer of the Faithful

Apart from reading the Scripture passages at Mass, it will some-times fall to a reader to lead the congregation in the Prayer of the Faithful, otherwise known as the Bidding Prayer.

This form of prayer originated in the prayers appended to the recitation of the psalms in the monastic celebration of the offices of Lauds and Vespers, the official morning and evening prayers of the Church. They have formed part of the Liturgy of the Word at Mass since the introduction of the new Roman Missal in 1974.

Their importance is that they offer an opportunity for active participation by the faithful in what, up to this point, has been largely a sanctuary-based activity. Further, it is here that inter-cession can be made for the felt contemporary needs of the community.

The purpose of the Bidding Prayer is to form a conclusion to the Liturgy of the Word. It draws together some of the key thoughts contained in or suggested by the readings and the homily, linking them to the cares and concerns of the worship-ping community. It forms, so to speak, a 'bridge' into the Lit-urgy of the Eucharist where all these concerns are united to the saving sacrifice of Christ.

The shape and form of the Prayer is outlined in the Roman Missal.

The Celebrant introduces the prayer, after which the Reader announces the intentions to be prayed for. This is important – strictly, the Reader is not, in this case, the person making the prayer; the praying is done by the congregation in the silence of their own hearts after the announcement of each intention.

When all the intentions have been prayed for, then the Celebrant offers up a concluding, summing-up prayer.

It follows that there should be an appreciable silence after each intention so as to allow the congregation to make their own prayers.

The end of each period of silent prayer may be marked by 'Lord, hear us: Lord, graciously hear us', or a similar phrase.

The range and type of the intentions are also suggested by the Roman Missal. They should normally cover four categories – the needs of the universal Church; public authorities and the salvation of the world; those who are oppressed or are facing any need; the needs of the local community. If possible, the petitions should be so phrased as to be relevant to the readings and homily which we have just heard. When it comes to the intentions of the local Church or parish, including those who are ill, or who have asked for prayers, it is important to note that the Prayer of the Faithful is not the place for long lists of names.

Both the Roman Missal and various other publications (some considerably better than others; select with care!) offer complete texts for the Bidding Prayer. Nevertheless, however eloquent such publications may be, it is better that the Prayer of the Faithful should be written specially for each Celebration.

Where this is done, however, great care should be paid to the form, language and underlying theology of the prayer. It would be quite wrong, for instance, for the reader to begin each intention with an address to 'Lord Jesus' or, indeed, to any other member of the Holy Trinity, let alone any of the saints. The task of the Reader here is simply to announce intentions, not to 'make prayers'.

In some parts of the English-speaking world, the custom has grown up of including the Hail Mary at the end of the Prayer of the Faithful. However, the practice is nowhere mentioned in the Missal, nor is it really appropriate within the Mass, where all prayers should be addressed directly to God the Father, through the Son and in the Holy Spirit.

As with any other reading, a good Bidding Prayer will have been well prepared by the Reader. From the nature of the case, however, it is possible that the text of the prayer will not be available early in the week for preparation at home. All the more important, then, for the Reader to be present in good time before Mass, so that the Bidding Prayer may be studied and possible pitfalls avoided.

FIFTEEN

Guide to pronunciation

Note: As written, Hebrew uses no vowels. Thus the name of God, for instance, is equivalently rendered JWH. This. as it stands is clearly unpronouncable. In Hebrew, the vowel sounds, while not written, were handed down by oral tradition. Modern research shows that the name of God was pronounced *Yah*-Weh and not, as some have surmised, JeHoVah. In the following guide, where there are alternatives, the pronounciation in common usage is given.

Aaron *Air*-on
Abiathar Ab-*ee*-athar
Aeneas Ay-*nay*-ass
Ananias An-an-*eye*-ass
Areopagus Arry-*op*-a-gus
Apocalypse A-*pock*-alips
Baruch Bar-*uck*
Beelzebub Bee-*el*-zibub
Bethsaida Beth-*side*-ah
Canaan *Kane*-an
Caparnaum Cap-*are*-na-um
Cappadocia Kappa-*doe*-chia
Colossians Kol-*oss*-ians
Dalmanutha Dal-man-*ooth*-a
Deuteronomy Dyou-ter-*on*-omy
Didymus *Diddy*-mus
Ecclesiastes Ek-lazy-*ass*-tays
Ecclesiastucus Ek-lazy-*ass*-ticus
Emmaus Em-*ah*-us or Em-*ay*-us

Eutychus Ey-*you*-ticus
Ezekiel Ez-*ee*-kiel
Gabbatha *Gab*-a-tha
Gamaliel Gam-*ey*-liel
Habakkuk *Hab*-a-kuk
Haceldama Hack-*el*-dama
Herodias Her-*ode*-ias
Herodion Her-*ode*-ion
Hezekiah Hez-eck-*eye*-ah
Illyricum Ill-*ir*-ikum
Isaiah Eye-*sigh*-ah
Joshua *Josh*-you-ah
Laodicea La-owe-di-*chay*-ah
Levite *Lee*-vite
Leviticus Lev-*it*-ikus
Lysias *Liss*-ias
Matthathias Matt-ah-*thigh*-ass
Naim Nah-eem
Nehemiah Nehm-hem-*eye*-ah
Onesimus Oh-*nay*-simus
Onesiphorus Oh-nay-*see*-for-us
Paralipomenon Para-lip-*om*-inon
Philemon Fill-*ay*-mon
Philippians Fill-*ipp*-ians
Phoenicia Phone-ee-*chee*-ay
Thessalonians Thess-a-*lone*-ians
Thessalonica Thess-a-*lon*-ika
Tychicus *Tyke*-i-cus
Uriah Your-*eye*-ah
Zechariah Zeck-are-*eye*-ah
Zorobabel Zo-*roe*-bab-el